A Blessed
Marriage

A Blessed Marriage

Senovia Wilson

© 2007 by Senovia Wilson. All rights reserved.

Cover design by Ufomadu Consulting & Publishing

Printed in the United States of America

No part of this publication may be reproduced, stored in a retrieval system, or transmitted in any way by any means—electronic, mechanical, photocopy, recording, or otherwise—without the prior permission of the copyright holder, except as provided by USA copyright law.

Scriptures references are taken from the King James Version of the Bible.

Published by:
Ufomadu Consulting & Publishing (UC&P)
P.O. Box 746
Selma, AL 36702-0746
www.UfomaduConsulting.com

ISBN-13: 978-0-9790022-0-5
ISBN-10: 0-9790022-0-6
LCCN: 2007924054

Dedication

This book is dedicated to single and married couples. This book was designed to promote spiritual marriages and break the cycle of traditional marriages.

"The couple that prays together stays together"

Matthew 19:6

"Wherefore they are no more twain, but one flesh. What therefore God hath joined together, let not man put asunder."

Introduction

God inspired me to write the book called *A Blessed Marriage* to help enhance and restore marriages. God motivated me to encourage young and old couples to establish a personal relationship with God before they get married. God placed a perfect word in my spirit to apply wisdom and knowledge about transforming marriages according to the word of God. God allowed me to go through different trials and tribulations in my marriage in order to plant a blessed seed back into the community, state, and throughout the world. God prepared me as a holy vessel in the ministry of marriage.

Through experience, I learned that without God in a relationship, the marriage is a **setup**. Without having a personal relationship with God, marriage is compared to the waves in the sea. The marriage is always **rocky** with good and bad times. When the waves go up, the relationship goes very well, but when the waves go down, the relationship goes down. The marriage is not set on a solid foundation but on watery land. However, there is a scripture that says if the

Lord does not build the house, then the laborers build in vain. Therefore, if **God** does not **build** the marriage, then the couple builds a relationship in vain.

I was inspired to write this book to bind up traditional routines, strongholds and generational cures off of marriages. I was designated to sow a seed by spreading biblical wisdom and testimonies to loose blessings upon marriages.

However, the purpose of writing this book is to distinguish between the lifestyle of a marriage when operating in sin and the lifestyle of a marriage transformed and converted to Christ. The rationale for this book is to testify how God allowed a marriage to decrease when the couple was walking in the flesh. But once the couple makes a transition to establish a personal relationship with God, the marriage begins to increase, transform, and be blessed. God restores the marriage. It's Restoration season! It is time for everyone to take back everything that the locust has eaten up. It is a new season to restore marriages.

Therefore, whatever has caused your marriage to go astray, the body of the church needs to bind it up in the name of Jesus. The season has come to receive a word from God to break the yoke off of marriages.

How Did it All Start?

The marriage was derived from an ultimatum. It was established when the wife proposed an ultimatum to the husband about marriage. The ultimatum was, "You either marry me or I am going to move on with my life," says the wife. However, the ultimatum was the wrong way to motivate or persuade someone to marry you. The couple realizes that if someone convinces or forces someone to do something that he or she is not ready to do then, the individuals are not going to be dedicated, committed, or effective in the relationship.

A Blessed Marriage

Many women are giving men an ultimatum to marry them for one reason after another. But, by proposing an ultimatum, it gives the devil the opportunity to gamble with your marriage. The devil knows that one of the individuals wants to be in a marriage while the other individual is undecided in his/her mind, but consents to marriage because of the ultimatum. The scriptures say that, *"The thief cometh not, but to steal, to kill, and to destroy: I am come that they might have life, and that they might have it more abundantly"* (John 10:10). The devil is seeking to kill, steal, and destroy marriages because he knows that when two people are joined together in marriage, there is power and unity as one flesh. God desires for married couples to be joined together as one flesh. However, Satan desires to separate married couples. Therefore, married couples need to have a relationship with God in order to conquer any battle, situation, or strong hold. So, the question is, "Will the married couple survive in this ultimatum marriage or get defeated by Satan?" Well, let's read on to find out what happens. Let's explore the things that happen the night **before the wedding**.

A Blessed Marriage

A Blessed Marriage

"The Night Before the Wedding"

Many couples have been bound up in a cycle of separating from their companion the night before the wedding. Many couples say traditionally that it is bad luck to see the bride or groom before the wedding. Many couples traditionally have a bachelor's party the night before the wedding. At the bachelor's party, many men and women engage in their **last dances**, **last drink**, **last smoke**, **last intimacy**, and **last pornography**. The men and women are engaged in entertainment of the flesh, which glorifies the devil. The devil speaks a voice in the men and women's ear and says, " You better do your sinful act for the **last time** because the wedding is tomorrow." The men and women satisfy their flesh because they feel as though they have to do everything for the last time before the wedding takes place. Many people do their last dirty deeds before the weeding. Consequently, the couple that became engaged because of an ultimatum experienced all of these trials the night before the wedding. The couple was unfocused and had the wrong interpretation of celebrating the night before the wedding.

However, this stronghold and yoke **the night before the wedding** has to be destroyed. It is not biblical to separate from your spouse the night before the wedding. Therefore, the saints of God need to motivate young couples to use their time wisely the night before the wedding and rebuke the devil when evil thoughts and imaginations try to linger around. The young couples need to do something constructive to avoid causing anyone any pain. The couple needs to complete unfinished tasks to make preparation for the wedding instead of being enticed by Delilah spirits and things of the flesh. There are three things that separate and distract the couple from God. These are the lust of the **flesh,** lust of the **eye**, and the **pride** of life. Many couples wrestle with putting their flesh under subjection to fulfill a **temporary feeling** that satisfies the flesh. This temporary feeling only lasts a few minutes; then it vanishes. Therefore, the question that married couples need to consider in their mind is, "Why destroy your relationship over a temporary feeling?" Also, many couples are enticed about what they see with the natural eye, such as lusting after women or men's outside beauty and body parts. The couple desires to become intimate with someone else outside of their marriage to receive a temporary feeling that can destroy the couple for a lifetime.

A Blessed Marriage

The Ultimatum Wedding

Now, on this special day in December, Mr. and Mrs. Doubtfire were joined together in a marriage at a Baptist Church. Oh, what a beautiful wedding it was! The decorations were teal and ivory. The bride's maids, matron, groomsmen, and best man were as sharp as a tack in their rented wedding attire.

However, the bride and the groom were going down the aisle without any Godly counseling and just messed up the night before the wedding. The couple was getting married with no guidance and no foundation. The lost lovers are in the process of making a commitment and marry without being knowledgeable of what a true comitment is all about. The young couple was portraying to be in love, but mentally, they were unable to discriminate between love and lust. The scripture says that God is love; therefore, if a man has not God, he has not love. Therefore, how can a man love an individual the way he/she needs to be loved without God? Now, there's an ungodly couple at the alter consenting to love one another for the rest of their lives. "Ha, Ha, Ha," laughs the devil, while he watches the couple set themselves up. The ungodly couple continues to repeat the vows after the preacher to promise to love, honor, and cherish each other for the rest of their lives.

A Blessed Marriage

However, the devil watches the couple make commitments in their vows and later tests the couple to see if they were going to bite the words that they consent to within the vows.

The Reception

The couple gets married and later has a worldly party to celebrate the ungodly wedding. The couple rejoices with **God** at the **church** and rejoices with the **devil** at the **reception**. The couple does not have a balanced marriage. The couple has a holy matrimony wedding and a "shake what your momma gave you" reception for the devil. But, God says in His word that people need to be hot or cold; but if you are lukewarm, then he will spew you out of his mouth. A relationship with partially God and partially the devil is a **unequilibrum** marriage. The couple needs to make a choice whether or

A Blessed Marriage

not they are going to serve God or Satan. The couple is confused and mixed up in their relationship. The couple is undecided about the lifestyle that they are going to live. Therefore, if the couple decides to choose life then they are entitled to a blessed and prosperous lifestyle, otherwise, if they choose death, then they have to suffer the consequences of life. Watch and observe the lifestyle of the married couple after the wedding has taken place.

A Blessed Marriage

The Lifestyle of the Married Couple

After the wedding, the young couple was still caught up in the old habit by walking in the flesh. The couple was hanging out with the same friends and doing the same worldly habits. The husband was hanging out with the homeboys in the club and the wife was hanging out with the home girls. The couple was dwelling in the path of the unrighteous and ungodly people. As the couple was dwelling in the path of the ungodly, the people of the world begin to seduce, persuade, and motivate the couple to do things outside the will of God. The homeboys motivate the married husband to drink, smoke, and chase after females. The husband was overtaken by the strongholds of sins and entice by Jezebel spirits. On the other side, the worldly people motivated the wife to drink and smoke. The couple was walking in the flesh and was won over by the people of the world. The scripture says walk not in the counsel of the ungodly, nor stand in the way of the wicked. Because of this, the couple goes through a phase of dwelling in the mist of sinners and their dreadful acts, and was overtaken by the lust of the flesh.

A Blessed Marriage

By walking in the flesh, the marriage began to fall apart. The lust and compassion began to depreciate. In the scriptures, God says that those that walk after the flesh do mind things of the flesh and those who walk after the spirit do mind things of the spirit. Therefore, the couple experiences trials and tribulation in their marriage because they were walking in the flesh and doing mind things of the flesh.

The wife begins to sit at home, stare at the walls, and watch the alarm clock waiting for her husband to come home. The wife stares out of the window with anger in her spirit wondering, "What time is he coming home?" The next morning around

A Blessed Marriage

4:00 a.m., the wife would hear a key opening the house door. Guess who is walking in the door? Yes, it was the wife's husband creeping into the house from his late night adventures. Out of anger, the wife begins to react on her feelings, gets in the flesh, and calls her husband everything but a child of God. The wife calls things just like they were instead of speaking life and praying for her husband. God says in his word that, *"Death and life are in the power of the tongue and they that love it shall eat the fruit thereof"* (Proverb 18:21). However, the wife begins to dig her husband deeper in a ditch by calling him out of his name. The wife begins to eat the fruit of her lips by

A Blessed Marriage

speaking curses over her husband's life. Whatever the wife speaks, her husband manifests that particular type of behavior. The wife begins to fight her husband and says cruel words to express the deep feelings inside and to fulfill the void that was missing in her life. As a result, the wife and husband were in an abusive relationship physically and verbally. The couple was very popular on the police scanner. The couple was assigned a police code from the policeman. Now, the devil sits back and laughs again. "Ha, Ha, Ha," in a deep voice. The devil laughs while the couple goes through the storm and rain. Remember, the devil's purpose is to destroy the marriage and break the unity.

Fed Up, Ready to Give Up! (Wife)

While going through the trials and tribulations, the wife was on the edge of giving up on the marriage. The wife was torn between a rock and a hard place. The wife begins to lose interest and love for her husband. She begins to have mental thoughts in her mind about getting even. She was very fed up with battling with Jezebel spirits and wanted a way out. The wife was fed up with crying and desired to search for happiness. The wife cries out with a loud voice, "I can't take this anymore!" She feels as though she needs to **drop that "zero"** and find her a **hero.** The wife feels as though there's a void missing in her life. She feels as though she has been seeking and searching for love in all the wrong places. Therefore, the wife creates a poem to express her innermost feelings.

Searching for a Holy Destiny

*When I open my eyes, I awake with no where to **turn***
*Because the stress and depression make my heart **burn***
*I searched and searched for a better **lifestyle***
*Knowing that my spirit was weaken like a lost little **child***
*Therefore, I begin to wonder through the wilderness with no map to **follow***
*I realize that I was missing a relationship with my heavenly **Father***
*I was fed up with the issues and tribulations of **life***

*Therefore, I was led to convert to **Christ**
So, searching for a Holy destiny was not bad at **all**
Transforming my life was a part of God's plan to restore me from the **fall***

A Blessed Marriage

Fed up with the Lifestyle, Ready to Change (Husband)

The husband was fed up with his life style. He was chastised by God through many different accidents. In one accident, the husband was leaving home and a man was coming down a hill asleep and crashed into the back of his car. Gas was leaking every where. This was the first day that God begins to chastise and warn the husband to change his sinful life around. God begins to speak to the husband and tell him that he is giving him time to get it right. God speaks again and says, "Son, if you live according to my commandments, then thy shall be blessed; otherwise, curses will be upon your life."

The husband was engaged in another car incident in front of his house. The husband was leaving home again and his son was bending down reaching for a cat. The husband placed the car in reverse and runs over his son unintentionally. The wife comes to the door and shouts,"Where is my son?" The husband stops the car and look underneath the car and his son was between the tires. The husband realizes that it was God who saved his sons' life again. The husband grabs his son from underneath the car with no scratches or bruises. The husband realizes that God has given him a second chance to change or something drastic was going to happen in his life.

Thankfully, the husband was very fearful of God's warnings and signs. The husband took heed to the warnings. He decided to live righteous so that he can live a blessed life. The husband was driven to make the transition, stop the sinful acts, and turn his life to Christ. He was fed up with his disobedience of God, and desired to make the transition to restore his family. Therefore, God began to change the husband's mentality about striving to live for Christ.

A Blessed Marriage

Changing the Husband

(Transformed)

After the husband realized that the wife was on the edge of giving up on the marriage, he apologizes with sorrow. The husband realized that he has to give up the strongholds or lose his wife. The husband began to confess his sinful acts. The husband began to confess that he was ready to change his life around and live for Christ. He began to attend a church in Alabama where he sought Godly counseling from the pastor and first lady of the church. He began to find himself striving to live righteous. He began to walk and talk like Christ. He began to honor his wife as a virtuous woman. He realized that the scripture says, *"Whoso findeth a wife, findeth a good thing and obtaineth favor with the Lord"* (Proverb 18:22). He realized that his wife's character lines up with the word of God in the category of a virtuous woman. The husband remembers the scripture, *"Who can find a virtuous woman? For her price is far above rubies. The heart of her husband doth safely trust in her so he shall have no need to spoil. She will do him good and not evil all the days of her life"* (Proverb 31:10-12).

"Oh my God," says the wife. "My husband is really changing." Later, the wife

A Blessed Marriage

begins to see a transition in her husband and decides to forgive him and remain in the marriage. The wife imagines in her mind that she wishes that she could turn back the hands of time and maybe situations would be a lot different. However, because the wife does not have the power to turn back the hand of time, she begins to accept the things that she cannot change. The wife learns to put the past behind her and focus on the future with her newly transformed husband in Christ Jesus. The wife remembers that in the movie *Women Thou Art Loosed,* T.D. Jakes focuses on the importance of laying **past experiences** and hurts on the alter and leave the heavy weight in the past. The wife realized that God forgives people "seven times seventy" and throws our sins in the sea of forgiveness. Therefore, the wife realized that she had to forgive her husband and place the past and hurt in the sea of forgiveness. The wife remembered a scripture that says, *"If any man be in Ch rist; he is a new creature; old things have passed away; behold all things become new"* (2 Corinthians 5:17). Therefore, the wife forgave her husband for the old things that he had done and accepted the newness of Christ. The wife denied pride and accusations that the world had to offer and accepted her **transformed** husband back into her heart. The wife realized that she needed a peace of mind and happiness. The wife also realized that it does not matter what the outside world thinks about her revitalizing the marriage, as long as she is happy and satisfied with her new creature. Therefore, the wife recognized that it was time for her to change.

A Blessed Marriage

Changing the Wife

Because the wife saw the sincerity and newness in her husband, it converts her to Christianity. The wife begins to read the Bible, attend church, and pray for her husband. The wife learns though the marriage's trials and tribulations to put her trust and confidence in God instead of man. The wife learns that a man is only human flesh; therefore, if a man walks after the flesh, he does mind things of the flesh. The wife remembered a scripture that says, "Those who walk after the flesh do mind things of the flesh; but those who walk after the spirit do mind things of the spirit."

Therefore, the wife learned to pray for her husband and trust God because he has power over the husband in making different decisions.

The wife begins to learn about God for herself. She learns the importance of putting God first in her life. The wife learns that she always had a relationship with God but she was not walking in the knowledge of CHRIST. Because the wife lacked the true knowledge of church during her childhood, she was under the impression that it was all right to commit sin as long as you attended church on Sunday. However, that was the wrong concept of church. The wife realizes through the wisdom of the Bible that people need to present their bodies a living sacrifice, holy and acceptable unto God. Therefore, people need to walk in the Spirit and live a righteous life. The wife realizes that if people walk in the Spirit then they will have a prosperous and blessed life. Therefore, the wife writes a poem to describe her new identity as a **changed woman**.

"A Changed Woman"

Saint is something that I have chosen to be
Eager to learn the word of God, you see
New creature is the nickname that I was called
Overwhelmed with blessing, I just can't tell
it all
Virtuous woman, that's who I am,
Individual sold out for Christ because I was
*in a **jam***
Awesome child, staying in the spiritual
realm.

New Beginning

Now, the husband and wife are collaborating, communicating, and living according to the word of God. The couple begins to walk in Christ together. The couple begins to lay aside the old lump and put on the new creation. They begin to attend church together in Tyler. They begin to live according to the Bible's commandments. The couple was sold out for Christ.

A Blessed Marriage

The Confession

Things begin to change for the married couple. The couple was beginning to find their true identity in the Lord. However, one Sunday, the preacher was preaching a message about calling their husband "**Lord**". Therefore, the wife stands up steadfast and calls her husband "Lord" because the relationship was improving and getting better. Meanwhile, after calling her husband 'Lord', the preacher suggests that all the married couples embrace each other at the church. Therefore, several women embrace their husband.

A Blessed Marriage

But, after returning home from church, the husband implies that he wants to talk to the wife about the preacher's message. The husband implies and confesses that he was not worthy to be called 'Lord'. The wife says, "Why do you think that you are not worthy to be called 'Lord'?" The husband replies that he does not feel worthy of being called 'Lord" because he was unfaithful **in the past** and dishonest. The husband confesses past relationships.

The wife was very astonished and bewildered. But, the wife was able to forgive her husband because the relationship was just beginning to make a transition. The wife realizes that there is nothing hidden in the dark, and that God will bring it to the light in **due season**. Even though the wife was in suspension of her husband's relationships in the past, she realizes that she is now married to a **new creature**. The wife realizes that God allows people to decrease so that he can bring in His increase. Sometimes in life, many people want the blessed marriage, but they do not want to **fall** (decrease) in the relationship in order for God to bless (increase) the relationship. The wife's relationship was ordained to **sour** in order for God to make it **sweet**. The wife realizes that it was a part of God's plan to allow the relationship to be **broken** so that He can **repair** it. She realizes that all things work together for the good of those that love the Lord. The wife realizes that the race is not given to the swift or to the strong but to the one that endures until the end. The wife believes that the focus is not about the marriage that God delivers or restores **first,** but as long as the marriage endures **until the end**. The wife believes that many people are so swift to give up during tough times, but God says that the battle is not yours; it is the Lords. Therefore, the couple needs to **stand still**, position themselves, and watch the move of the God.

Birthing a Ministry

After the confession and breaking the yoke, the husband begins to walk closer to God. The husband was called into the ministry and delivered from the devil. The husband is now a born again new creature in Christ Jesus. He has established his own ministry. He was assigned to establish a ministry in the same neighborhood that he had done his dirty deeds. Therefore, the husband was predestined to save souls and plant seeds about the word of God to many people that he use to hang out with. The husband was obligated to clean up the community and allow his light to shine before men so that people could see his good works and glorify the Father, which is in heaven. The husband transforms a building from a club and turned it into a church. Once upon a time, the husband was dancing, distributing drugs, and playing games in the same building. However, God has **flipped the script** and now, the husband is dancing for the Lord, praying, shouting, and lifting up holy hands in the sanctuary. The husband has done a 180° turnaround to sow good seeds back into the community. God has allowed the husband to create a Godly community and restore everything that the devil had once stolen. Now, the drug dealers, alcoholics, and other sinners are being transformed and delivered in the community.

Restoration

After being called into the ministry, God placed different Christians in our lives to sow seeds about putting God in a marriage. Many Christians motivated the couple by saying **"the couple that prays together stays together."** Therefore, the couple applied the word of God toward their lives to defeat the enemy. The couple realized that *'No weapon that is formed against them shall prosper."* (Isaiah 54:17) Therefore, God restored the couple's marriage. The married couple created a **new love**, **interest, and compassion** for each other.

The wife realizes that because she did not give up her marriage, God has given her peace, joy, and happiness. The wife realizes that she is no longer bound with depression, but she is free from allowing the devil to kill, steal, and destroy her joy. The wife realizes through experience that the race is not given to the **swift** or to the **strong,** but the one that **endures until the end**. The wife endured until the end and she did not throw in the towel on her marriage. The wife sought Godly counseling to help her endure in the marriage. The wife realizes that the marriage is not based upon who conquers the challenging tasks first, but it is about enduring the challenging times.

Decrease Brings on an Increase (Summary of the Story)

Now, as you can see, the couple went through a state of decrease in their life when they were a part of the world. The couple went through a heartbreaking attack from the enemy. The couple suffered in their relationship because they both chose to walk in the flesh. The couple dealt with different obstacles, battles, and issues of the world. The couple fought with portraying a worldly identity. The couple wandered in the wilderness trying to find themselves and fulfill a void. The couple wandered in a circle facing problems after problems. The couple watched their lifestyle be empowered by Satan. In the marriage, it seemed like nothing was going right for the married couple. It seemed as though different evil spirits were trying to destroy the marriage. The couple began to decrease and fall.

Then the couple goes through a state of increase in their life when they convert to Christ. When the couple turns their life around, God really begins to bless the relationship. The couple prospers in their relationship when they begin to walk in the spirit. The couple begins to become honest, faithful, and obedient to each other. The couple's relationship is now on a solid foundation instead of rocky, like that waves in the sea. The couple began to speak to the waves and said, "**Peace be Still,**" and peace was still. The married couple realized that God has a way of bringing about peace, even if He has to allow you to fall. A just man falls seven times, but he gets back up again. Now, the relationship is on the rise and God has taken the married couple to another level in Christ Jesus. So, the question is, "Did the ultimatum wedding survive?" Yes, the ultimatum wedding survived, but the couple experienced transformation and isolation in order for God to give them **elevation**. Now, the married couple experiences a true and Godly relationship as lovers and friends.

A True Relationship (My Lover, My Friend, My Spouse)

God has shaped and molded the couple together to be unified as lovers, friends, and 'my other half'. God has given the couple the opportunity to learn about each other's personalities, differences and true identity. God has reveled to the couple that a true relationship requires the husband and wife to be a friend, lover, and partner to each other.

The husband and wife need to be a **lover** to each other. A lover is a person who is faithful and makes a commitment to the love of his/her heart. The lover imparts the inner love into his/her mate. The lover has warm affections toward his/her mate even when the husband or wife is not in the mood. The couple engages in a spiritual and physical intimacy and receives a temporary feeling that last forever until eternity. The couple remembers one of their favorite bible verses that says, *"Your body does not belong to you but to your husband."* (1Cor. 7: 3-5) Therefore, even when you are not in the mood for making love, the husband or wife has to deny himself /herself and commit to their lover. The word of God also states that the bed is **undefiled**. Therefore, the husband and wife have the opportunity to **explore intimacy with their own creativity**. Oh my, oh my, what a wonderful feeling it is to show affection and love toward someone that is in you heart. Can you just remember the first time you ever received your **climax** after intimacy with your spouse? Oh, what a connection and bond the husband and wife feel during the creative moment. The angels are smiling down on the couple observing as the couple produces holy fruit and multiply.

The husband and wife need to be a **friend** to each other. A friend presents himself/herself friendly. A friend is a person who has strong liking and trust in another person. A friend opens up a door to communicate and collaborate with decision-making. A friend confers each other in the time of need and prays for one another when in distress.

The husband and wife also need to be a **spouse** to each other. A spouse is a person who is a lawful husband or wife. The spouse makes a commitment based upon the covenant of Jesus Christ.

Godly Advice Before Getting Married

In conclusion of this book, my goal is to contribute Godly advice before the couple gets married. Through trials and tribulations of marriage, I realize it is very important to learn from your experience and apply the new Godly strategies to prevent previous mistakes. Therefore through the experience, I learn that both partners need to **establish a personal relationship with God** before marriage because if a man does not have God, then he does not have LOVE. Therefore, how can a man in the flesh love a person the way he/she needs to be loved without God? God is the root and vine of the marriage. Therefore, without the root and branch, the relationship decreases from growing and sprouting out.

God also warns his people about couples who marry **unequally yoked**. God recognizes that the end results of unequally yoked marriages are destruction. Therefore, believers need to marry someone of the same faith. The scripture says, *'Be ye not unequally yoked together with unbelievers: for what fellowship hath righteousness with unrighteousness? And what communion hath light with darkness?"* (2 Corinthians 6:14). Therefore, please allow the Lord to send someone that the wife or husband can touch and agree with in the marriage. The scripture says, *'Can two walk together except they agree?"* (Amos 3:3). Otherwise, one person is going to walk in the flesh while the other partner walks in the Spirit. The Godly marriages need to use more synonyms than antonyms to explicitly describe the relationship. Synonyms have the same meaning, which signifies unity, whereas antonyms have the opposite meaning, which signifies disarray or confusion. However, God is not the author of confusion, but of peace. Therefore, if you desire peace in your marriage, *'Seek ye first the Kingdom of God and everything shall be added unto you.*

(Matthew 6:33).

A Blessed Marriage

Scriptures for A Blessed Marriage

"Enjoying Intimacy at all times unless Fasting and Praying"

Corinthians 7: 4-5

"The wife hath not power of her own body, but the husband: and likewise also the husband hath not power of his own body, but the wife" (Corinthians 7:3). It is relevant that the husband and wife render to each other to fulfill their sexual desires. It is so important that the husband and wife have a personal and physical relationship to express their innermost feelings. When the husband and wife compress together and become

intimate with each other, they connect their unity in their mind, body, and soul. Therefore, when the climax comes, it feels like the Holy Ghost has overtaken the couple to produce an awesome relaxing product. Therefore, *'Defraud ye not one the other, except it be with consent for a time that ye may give yourselves to fasting and prayer; and come together again, that Satan tempt you not for your incontinency"* (Corinthians 7:4). It is so important to collaborate together and inform your spouse if an individual is preparing to fast and pray. Otherwise, the husband and wife do not need to make excuses to avoid intimacy with their spouse. Some excuses that couples use to avoid intimacy are, "I'm tired," or, "One of my body parts ache."

"Be Submissive Toward your Husband or Wife"

Ephesians 5:21-23

The scripture says that the husband and wife need to submit themselves, one to another, in the fear of God. In order to have a blessed marriage, the couple needs to be very submissive toward one another, that they fear the consequences and chastisement of God.

"Wives, submit yourselves unto your own husbands, as unto the Lord" (Ephesians

5:22). The wife is ordered by God to submit herself unto her husband only. Therefore, the wife does not need to commit adultery or lust after someone else's property. The wife needs to be dedicated, committed, and faithful to her husband with her mental thoughts, body parts, and heart. The scripture also states that the husband is the head of the wife, even as Christ is the head of the church. This scripture simply means that the husband is the leader over the wife, just as God is the leader over the husband. The husband's job is to lead and guide his family according to the word of God. The husband has certain guidelines to lead his family through financial support, spiritual guidance, and in making decisions. The husband is not authorized to physically abuse, or make all decisions by himself. The husband has a special calling on his life to keep things in order, based upon the standards of Christ.

"Never Ending Marriage" Matthew 19:6

God has commanded the married couples to stay joined together as one flesh. God specifies in His word that, *'Wherefore they are no more twain, but one flesh; what therefore God hath joined together, let not man put asunder"* (Matthew 19:6). However the scripture reveals that when

A Blessed Marriage

God places a couple together into a holy marriage, nothing causes the couple to depart from each other. The Godly couple is no longer twain (two), but one flesh unified together. Therefore, hard times, tribulations, sickness, lack of communication or distress does not need to intervene between the relationship of the wife and husband. God gives Godly couples the power to endure any situation. The Lord does not put anymore on Christians couples than they are able to bear. The word of God says that believers are more than conquerors.

On the other hand, if God does not combine or join the couple together then the marriage ends up falling apart. Therefore, many couples give their spouse a documentation decree of divorce because the couple does not have strength to bear the heat when the kitchen gets too hot. The ungodly couple does not have power to resist temptation and the fleshly things of the word. However, couples need to consult God and get permission before consenting to marriage. The couple does not need to react on the flesh and choose a wife or husband based upon appearance or finances. Therefore, please couples, be lead by the Spirit and allow God to send that special person in your life.

Scriptures to Support a Healthy Marriage

I. Faithful
II. Submissive
III. Eternal Marriage

Faithful
1 Timothy 3:11-12

*Even so must their wives be grave, not slanderers, sober, **faithful** in all things.*

Let the deacons be the husbands of one wife, ruling their children and their own house well.

Submissive
Ephesians 5:21-23

Submitting yourselves one to another in the fear of God.

Wives, submit yourselves unto your own husbands, as unto the Lord.

For the husband is the head of the wife, even as Christ is the head of the church.

Marriage is for Life! (Eternal)

"A bond that should not be broken"

Matthew 19:6

Wherefore they are no more twain, but one flesh. What therefore God hath joined together, let not man put asunder.

About the Author

*Senovia Wilson is the author of "**A Blessed Marriage**." Senovia is a first grade teacher at Sophia P. Kingston Elementary School in Selma, Alabama. She has been teaching for six years. She has a Master's degree in Early Childhood education, Bachelor of Arts degree, and certification in Administration. She is also pursuing a National Board Certification as an Early Childhood Generalist.*

Senovia Wilson is married to Minister Eric Wilson. She has been happily married for 9 years. She is planning to renew her marriage vows in December 2007. She is excited that God has transformed her marriage to be an inspiration to people in the world.

She has four children: Eric, Derrick, Erion and Derrion Wilson. The author was born and raised in Selma, Alabama. Senovia is the daughter of Collins and Geraldine Barley.

Acknowledgements

I acknowledge God for inspiring me to write this book on marriage. I also acknowledge my husband for being my comforter, friend, and companion. I acknowledge my four children, Eric, Derrick, Erion, and Derrion for giving me strength to keep pressing on. I acknowledge my spiritual father Pastor Effell Williams for promoting my spiritual growth. I acknowledge

Pastor P.E. Bonner and Carroll Bonner for planting a seed towards spiritual growth and inspiration in my marriage. I acknowledge my mother, Geraldine Barley, and father, Collins Barley, for implanting me with the values needed for a wholesome and spiritual life. I acknowledge Dr. Udo F. Ufomadu who inspired me to write ***A Blessed Marriage***. *I acknowledge Romonia Hardy, one of my favorite cousins, who prophesized to me that one day I was going to publish a book* *after I had written a poem about marriage. She spoke a blessing into my life. Thankfully, the prophecy manifested itself. She reminded me of a scripture: "Death and Life are in the power of the tongue" (Proverbs 18:21).*

NOTES

NOTES

NOTES

NOTES

NOTES

www.ingramcontent.com/pod-product-compliance
Lightning Source LLC
Chambersburg PA
CBHW031300290426
44109CB00012B/656